Rock Hunters

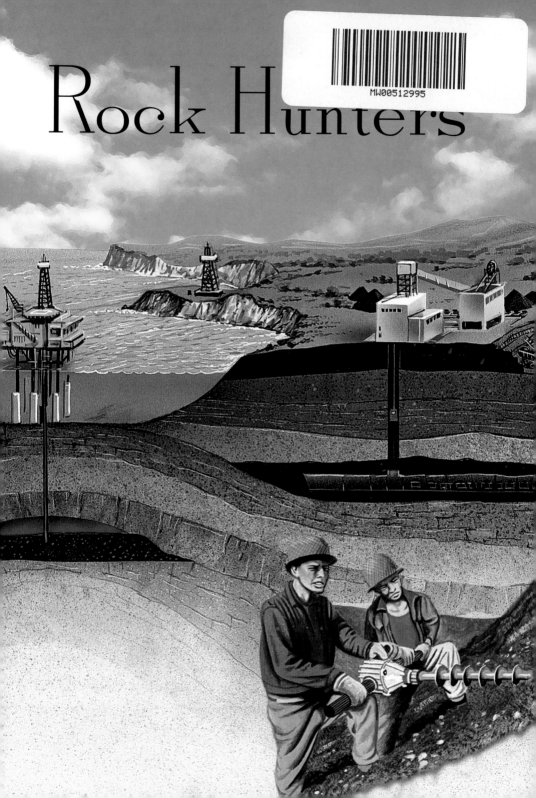

Contents

Features

Why does the word *crystal* come from a word meaning "ice"? Find out on page 6.

How was copper mined in Egypt long ago? The answer is on page 8.

Why is safety so important at a nuclear power plant? See page 15.

Learn how to make a fantastic rock collection in **Be a Rock Hound** on page 20.

Can you identify the rocks in your collection?

Visit **www.rigbyinfoquest.com** for more about **ROCKS.**

Where Would We Be Without Rock?

We may not notice it, but no matter where we are on Earth, rock is all around us. Mountains and hills are formed from rock. Soil and sand are made of rock that has been ground down over millions of years. Roads and buildings are made with rock. Trains, airplanes, and cars use **fuel** that is found inside some kinds of rock. We even use rock in our cooking. It's called salt!

Modern buildings are made of steel, concrete, and glass, which are made from rock.

Rock Salt

4

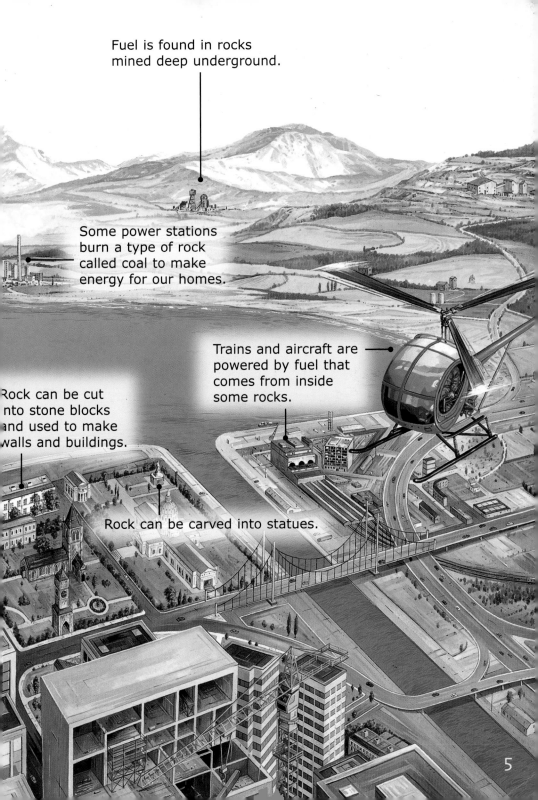

Fuel is found in rocks
mined deep underground.

Some power stations
burn a type of rock
called coal to make
energy for our homes.

Trains and aircraft are
powered by fuel that
comes from inside
some rocks.

Rock can be cut
into stone blocks
and used to make
walls and buildings.

Rock can be carved into statues.

5

Mighty Minerals

Look closely at a rock and you will see that it is made up of many tiny pieces. These tiny pieces are called **minerals.** The rocks in Earth's crust are made of thousands of different minerals. Some minerals, such as diamonds, grow to form large, beautiful **crystals.**

Some of Earth's most valuable minerals are **gemstones.** Gemstones can be cut and polished into sparkling jewels.

WORD BUILDER

The word *crystal* comes from the Greek word *crystallos*, meaning "ice." Long ago, the people in Greece believed that pieces of quartz, which are made of thousands of crystals, were actually water that was frozen so hard it wouldn't melt!

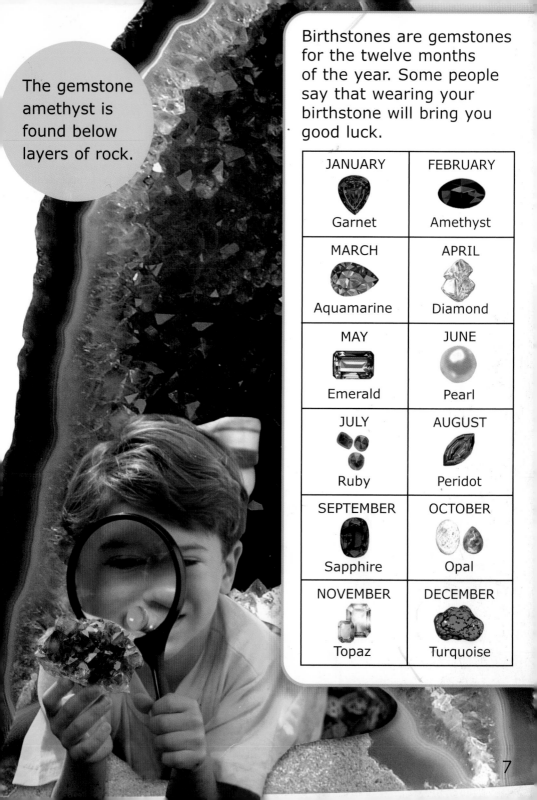

The gemstone amethyst is found below layers of rock.

Birthstones are gemstones for the twelve months of the year. Some people say that wearing your birthstone will bring you good luck.

JANUARY	FEBRUARY
Garnet	Amethyst
MARCH	APRIL
Aquamarine	Diamond
MAY	JUNE
Emerald	Pearl
JULY	AUGUST
Ruby	Peridot
SEPTEMBER	OCTOBER
Sapphire	Opal
NOVEMBER	DECEMBER
Topaz	Turquoise

Hidden Treasures

Earth is rich with minerals. Useful minerals that are dug from the ground, or mined, are called ores. Copper was one of the first ores ever mined. It can sometimes be found as a pure metal, not mixed with other minerals. Pure gold and silver are also found. Most metals, however, are mixed with other minerals in rock. It took people thousands of years to learn how to separate metal from rock.

TIME LINK

In Egypt long ago, copper was mined by sprinkling a crushed green stone over burning charcoal. The coppersmiths kept the fire hot by blowing air through long pipes. When the furnace was cool, black lumps at the bottom were smashed open. Tiny balls of copper were found inside.

Gold is a soft metal that is easily shaped into beautiful jewelry.

Today, most gold is mined by blasting through rock. However, gold can still be found in some rivers as it was many years ago. These children are "panning" for gold in a river.

9

Building Blocks

For thousands of years, people have used Earth's rock for building. Long ago, Egyptians cut limestone from **quarries** to build pyramids. The Romans and Greeks built beautiful stone temples and huge stadiums. In Central America, the Maya people used large stone blocks to build temples and tombs. The Chinese made the world's longest wall. Many of these structures still stand today.

Today, people use sand to make glass, and crush rock for cement. They use glass, cement, and steel to build modern apartments and other buildings.

Egyptian Pyramids

Roman Colosseum, Italy

Great Wall of China

In Central America long ago, the Maya people built huge stone temples.

Rocks for Fuel

Coal and oil are buried in layers of rock below Earth's surface. These fuels let us light our homes, cook our meals, keep warm, and travel. Coal comes from plants that have been pressed between layers of rock. Over many years, the plants turn into hard, black rock. The harder the coal, the more energy it gives off when it is burned.

The miners dig tunnels through the rock.

WORD BUILDER

Oil and gas are petroleum products. The word *petroleum* comes from the Latin words *petro,* meaning "stone," and *oleum,* meaning "oil."

Mining for Coal

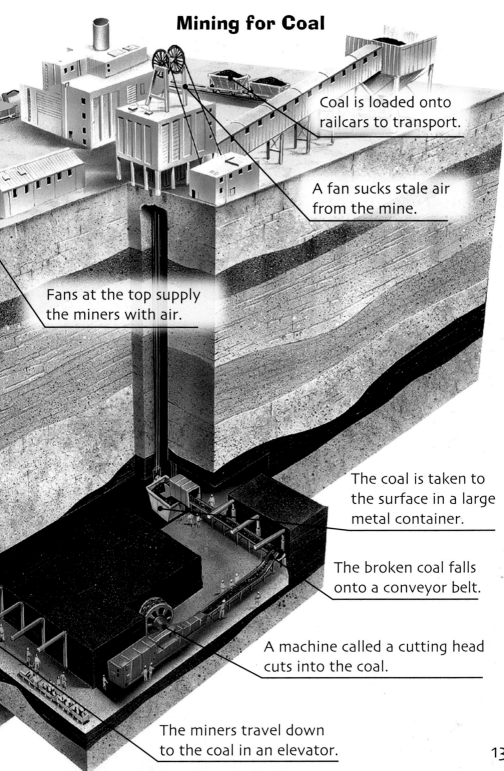

Coal is loaded onto railcars to transport.

A fan sucks stale air from the mine.

Fans at the top supply the miners with air.

The coal is taken to the surface in a large metal container.

The broken coal falls onto a conveyor belt.

A machine called a cutting head cuts into the coal.

The miners travel down to the coal in an elevator.

Nuclear Energy

Earth's supplies of coal, gas, and oil will not last forever. Because of this, people are finding other sources of energy. One source is nuclear energy, which is now used in many countries to provide electricity.

To produce nuclear energy, rock containing the metal uranium is used. When the **atoms** in uranium are split apart, energy is released. This energy is turned into power at nuclear power stations.

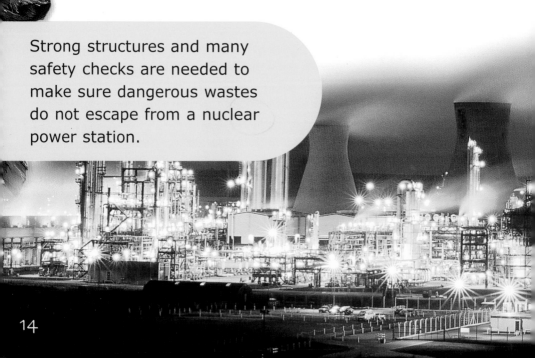

Strong structures and many safety checks are needed to make sure dangerous wastes do not escape from a nuclear power station.

Daily News • Saturday, April 26, 1986

Reactor Explodes!

In the early hours of this morning, there was a huge explosion at the Chernobyl nuclear power station in the Soviet Union.

Operators who were checking the fourth reactor noticed there was something wrong. They began an emergency shutdown.

Just seven seconds after the shutdown was started, the reactor exploded.

Fire and steam burst into the air, and clouds of poisonous radioactive material blew westward. People living west of Chernobyl should stay indoors to keep away from poisons in the air.

Chips of Rock

Technology has helped people find new ways to use rock. In the 1880s, two scientist brothers, Jacques and Pierre Curie, found that quartz produces electricity when it is squeezed. Today, quartz is used in clocks and watches. Some very strong materials are made by combining substances from rocks and minerals with new materials made by people. These materials are used to build many things, including spacecraft, skateboards, tennis rackets, and skis.

1

Graphite is a soft, greasy mineral that is used to make many things. It is lightweight but tough. It is mixed with clay to make pencil lead. It is also used in sports equipment such as tennis rackets, skis, and snowboards. It makes the equipment easy to use and bendable.

Space shuttles are built with many materials made from rocks and minerals.

1. The nose has *carbon* that can stand heat.
2. The windows have a *diamond* coating to stop scratching.
3. *Aluminum* is used in the frame. It is lightweight but strong.
4. The edges of the wings are covered with *carbon.*
5. A *titanium* heat shield is used on the outside of the shuttle to protect the steering equipment.

Digging for Answers

People who study rocks are called **geologists.**
Geologists are like detectives. They dig
throughout the world, searching for clues
to Earth's past. They also watch the changes
that are happening to Earth today.

Geologists drill into ocean floors. They keep
track of earthquakes to know what happens
underground. They watch volcanoes.
They use microscopes to examine rocks
and minerals, and they take photos of Earth
from space.

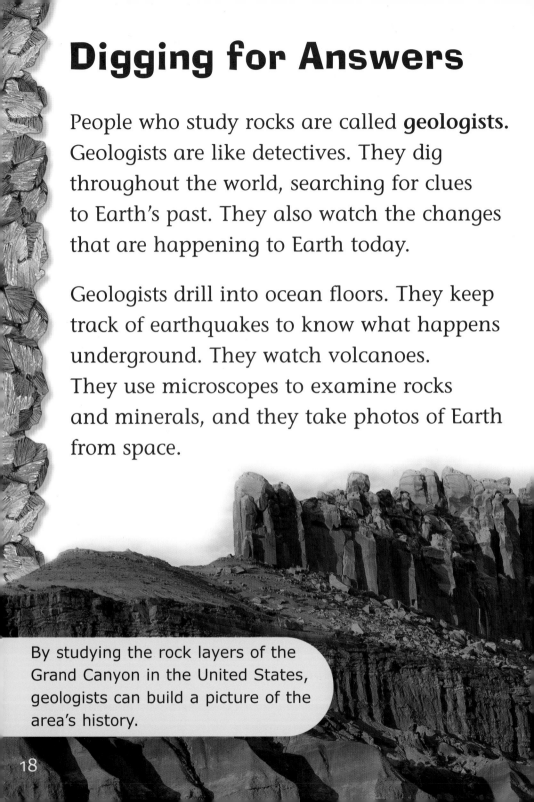

By studying the rock layers of the
Grand Canyon in the United States,
geologists can build a picture of the
area's history.

A geologist has even been sent to the moon. Astronaut and geologist H. Jack Schmitt landed on the moon in December 1972. He collected rock samples that showed there had been earthquakes and exploding volcanoes on the moon.

How Rock Is Formed

1

IGNEOUS ROCK
When a volcano explodes, hot liquid rock, or magma, breaks through Earth's surface. When magma flows onto the surface, it is called lava. Magma and lava cool to become igneous rock.

2

METAMORPHIC ROCK
Deep inside Earth's crust, pressure can change the shape of rock, and heat can change it from one kind of rock into another. The changed rock is called metamorphic rock.

3

SEDIMENTARY ROCK
Erosion breaks rock into tiny pieces that are carried into lakes and oceans. They become layers of sedimentary rock.

Be a Rock Hound

It is easy to become a rock hound by collecting and studying rocks. You can search for rocks just about anywhere. When you find a rock that interests you, make a note of where you found it. Draw the rock and the area you got it from. Clean and number your rock. You can sort your rocks by where you found them or how they look.

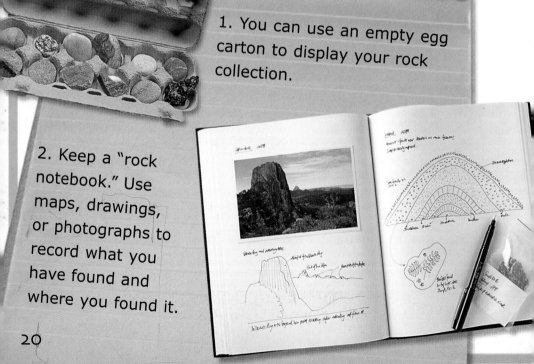

1. You can use an empty egg carton to display your rock collection.

2. Keep a "rock notebook." Use maps, drawings, or photographs to record what you have found and where you found it.

20

Put On a Show

Be proud to show your rock collection as museums do. After all, it's hard work collecting rocks.

1. Write labels telling where and when you found each rock.

2. Use shelves or drawers to display your samples.

3. Study your rocks with a magnifying glass.

4. Put breakable rocks in separate boxes.

Glossary

atom – one of the tiny bits, or particles, of which all things are made

crystal – one piece of a mineral that has a regular shape. Most things that are not living are made of crystals. Salt and other minerals, sugar, and snow are all made of crystals.

fuel – something that is burned to give heat or power. Coal, oil, and gas are fuels that are found buried in rock.

gemstone – any mineral or rock that can be cut and polished to be a jewel

geologist – a scientist who studies rocks. Geologists watch the changes that happen to Earth, both every day and over time.

mineral – a solid material found in Earth's crust that was never a plant or an animal

quarry – a place where stone is dug, cut, or blasted out of the ground

Index

Discussion Starters

1 Earth has many hidden treasures called gemstones. Can you think of any colored stones that you have seen made into jewelry? Do you know the names of any of the stones?

2 Do you know that in the 1800s, children as young as ten worked in coal mines? The work then was mostly done by hand, not with machines. Look at the illustration on page 13 and talk about the jobs miners in the 1800s might have had.

3 The world's supplies of oil are running out. However, oil from your car, truck, or lawnmower can be recycled. Do you think recycling this type of oil is a good idea? Why or why not?